# THE FINGERPRINT OF GOD!

## DAY 3

## Papa & Mama Goose

THE FINGERPRINT OF GOD – DAY 3

Papa & Mama Goose

Copyright © 2020
Enchanted Rose Publishing
P.O. Box 991
Hempstead, TX 77445

Published by Enchanted Rose Publishing
Layout by Cynthia D. Johnson @
www.diverseskillscenter.com

Written by Papa & Mama Goose

Printed in the United States of America
ISBN-13:

GOD's mercy endures forever.

By great wisdom, GOD raised-up the land above the water.

GOD said, "Gather the water below the sky in one place and let the dry land appear."

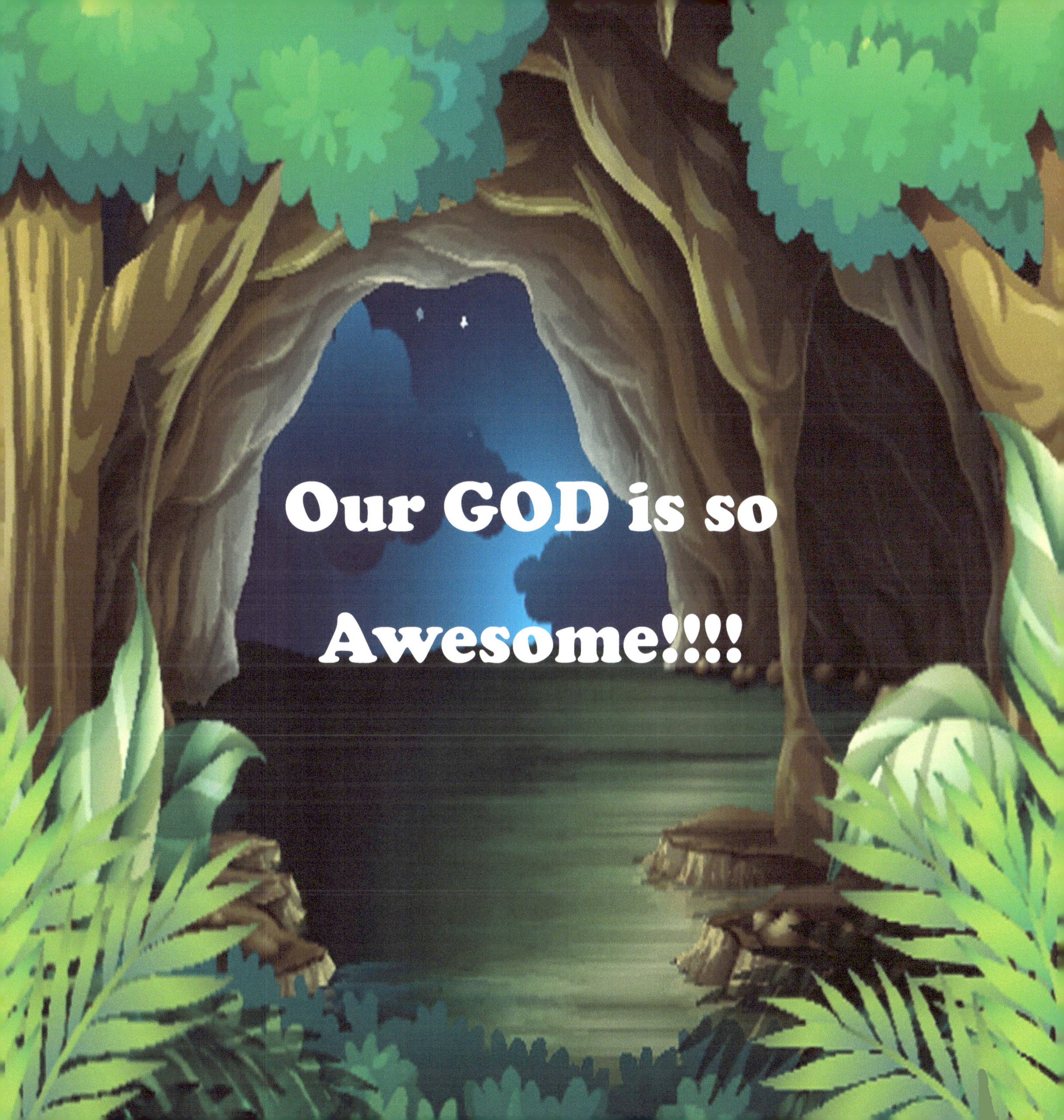

Our GOD is so

Awesome!!!!

GOD's great power and might was on full display.

GOD created all things for His purpose.

GOD called the land
Earth and the water
Seas.

Surprisingly, GOD did not want to end Day 3 yet!

Did you know that only GOD can create a seed?

While man can grow crops from seeds, he does not possess the ability to produce a seed from nothing.

When GOD created His special seedbearing plants, they shared a special relationship.

GOD gave the plants a molecular structure called DNA.

The DNA tells the plant what they will look like and how they will function.

GOD wanted to beautify the earth with the most beautiful plants and trees.

Consequently, the seedbearing plants had a multiplicity of roles.

For one, plants take in carbon dioxide to make oxygen.

As humans, we breathe in oxygen and breathe out carbon dioxide.

Theoretically, plants and humans would one day co-exist.

Plants and fruit would also provide food for animals and humans.

Humans would later use plants for medicinal purposes.

GOD also made the grass come out of the soil.

Have you ever noticed a tree or a wheat field during a gentle breeze?

They appear to be bowing and praising the goodness of GOD.

So, if all creation praises Him, so will I.

THE FINGERPRINT OF GOD – DAY 3

Written by Papa & Mama Goose

Copyright 2020

by

Mama Goose Books

Hempstead, Texas

## Papa & Mama Goose Media

**Follow Me On…**

 Facebook

www.facebook.com/goma
magoose

 Twitter

@GoMamaGoose

 Instagram

MamaGoose Paris

gomamagoose@gmail.com

Through the power of their faith and instructions from GOD's HOLY SPIRIT, these humble servants of CHRIST take us back to our beginning...The Bible. Although Papa and Mama Goose have written a plethora of books, none can hold a candle to how the WORD of GOD has guided their lives. Realizing that life on Earth is temporal, Papa and Mama Goose wanted to write Books about the Bible that would provide a Biblical Foundation for young children. The goal of the books is to teach youngsters to know and fall deeply in Love with GOD.

It was during their years in college that Papa and Mama Goose found CHRIST. They were taught the Gospel and baptized into the Prairie View CHURCH of CHRIST at Prairie View A & M University in Prairie View, Texas. Papa and Mama Goose enjoy sharing the same spiritual birthday. Currently, the dynamic duo are faithful members of the Fifth Ward CHURCH of CHRIST in Houston, Texas.